The World's *Stupidest* Laws

David Crombie

Michael O'Mara Humour

First published in Great Britain in 2000 by
Michael O'Mara Books Limited
9 Lion Yard
Tremadoc Road
London SW4 7NQ

www.mombooks.com

Copyright © 2000 by Michael O'Mara Books Ltd

All rights reserved. No part of this publication may be
reproduced, stored in a retrieval system, or transmitted by
any means, without the prior permission in writing of the
publisher, nor be otherwise circulated in any form of binding
or cover other than that in which it is published and without
a similar condition including this condition being imposed
on the subsequent purchaser.

The right of David Crombie to be identified as the author of
this work has been asserted by him in accordance with the
Copyright, Designs and Patents Act 1988.

A CIP catalogue record for this book is available from the
British Library

ISBN 1-85479-549-X

18 17 16 15 14 13 12

Designed and typeset by K DESIGN, Winscombe, Somerset

Printed and bound in Great Britain by Cox & Wyman, Reading, Berks.

Introduction

In the mid-1980s I was appointed a magistrate sitting on the Salisbury bench in Wiltshire. For a year or so I was quite content in my position until the problem of access to Stonehenge during the summer solstice reared its ugly head in Salisbury and the surrounding district. Basically, for those of you who do not know the story, the hippies and travelling folk wanted to celebrate the solstice at the stones, but ancient laws were dragged up to stop them doing this. Because of the number of arrests, special court sittings were introduced and I spent a number of valuable days listening to prosecuting counsel explain why some obscure law of 300 years ago had been broken.

During this time I started to think to myself that some of these laws were REALLY STUPID. Some of the days in court became a farce and I soon became disenchanted with the whole system and resigned. I did, however, retain my interest in stupid laws and have been an avid collector ever since. I hope you find this book informative, as well as humorous.

I would like to thank everyone who has helped me in my research, especially Eliza Kennedy and Suzanne Paterson. I would also like to mention my two daughters, Kate and Caroline, who have just informed me that it is against the law for me to enter their bedroom. And lastly, a big thank you to my editor, Helen Cumberbatch, who apart from doing a great job, also amazed me by knowing of John Shuttleworth, the versatile singer-songwriter from Sheffield. Now there is a man I should write a book about!

David Crombie, Dorking, Surrey
July 2000

We have several set forms which are held as law, and so held and used for good reason, though we cannot at present remember that reason.

Chief Justice Fortescue, 1458

Quips from the Courtroom

JUDGE TO THE JURY: Now, as we begin, I must ask you to banish all present information and prejudice from your minds, if you have any.

Friction in the Family

Q What is your brother-in-law's name?

A Jones.

Q What is his first name?

A I can't remember.

Q He has been your brother-in-law for forty years, and you can't remember his first name?

A No, I tell you, I'm too excited. [He then stands up and points to his brother-in-law.] For God's sake Sam, tell them your first name!

Q What is the first thing your husband said to you in the morning when he woke?

A He said, 'Where am I, Kathy?'

Q And why did that upset you?

A My name is Susan.

5

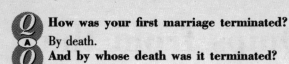

Q How was your first marriage terminated?

A By death.

Q And by whose death was it terminated?

Q What is your relationship with the plaintiff?

A She is my daughter.

Q Was she your daughter on 13 February, 1979?

Q Mr Slattery, you went on a rather elaborate honeymoon, didn't you?

A I went to Europe, sir.

Q And you took your new wife?

Q Was it you or your brother that was killed in the war?

Q Please state the nature of your relationship to the minor child.

A I'm his mother.

Q And you have been so all of his life?

Q What is your name?

A Emily McDowell.

Q And what is your marital status?

A Fair.

6

Do you know if your daughter has ever been involved in voodoo or the occult?

We both do.

Voodoo?

We do.

You do?

Yes, voodoo.

 Are you married?

No, I'm divorced.

And what did your husband do before you divorced him?

A lot of things I didn't know about.

 She had three children, right?

Yes.

How many were boys?

None.

Were there any girls?

 I understand you are Ted Funnel's mother?

Yes.

How long have you known the defendant?

7

Q Your foster son, Michael – who cooks for him?

A Oh, I do.

Q How often do you cook for him?

A We have probably one good meal a week.

Q Well, no commentary on your cooking, but how many bad meals do you have?

Q How many times have you beaten up your wife?

A Never. I might slap her around a bit.

Q Do you have any children or anything of that kind?

Q So the date of conception was 8 August?

A Yes.

Q What were you and your husband doing at the time?

Dumb Dialogue
with Doctors

Q Doctor, before you performed the autopsy, did you check for a pulse?

A No.

Q Did you check for blood pressure?

A No.

Q Did you check for breathing?

A No.

Q So, then it is possible that the patient was alive when you began the autopsy?

A No.

Q How can you be so sure, Doctor?

A Because his brain was sitting on my desk in a jar.

Q But could the patient have still been alive nevertheless?

Q How did you happen to go to Dr Murray?

A Well, a woman down the road had had several of her children by him, and said he was really good.

Q Doctor, did you say he was shot in the woods?

A No, I said he was shot in the lumbar region.

Q **Doctor, as a result of your examination of the plaintiff, is the young lady pregnant?**

A The young lady is pregnant, but not as a result of my examination.

Q **Do you recall the time that you examined the body?**

A The autopsy started around 8.30 p.m.

Q **And Mr Hubert was dead at the time?**

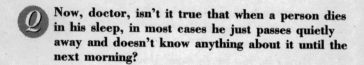

Q **Now, doctor, isn't it true that when a person dies in his sleep, in most cases he just passes quietly away and doesn't know anything about it until the next morning?**

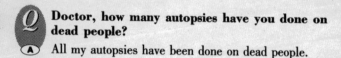

Q **Doctor, how many autopsies have you done on dead people?**

A All my autopsies have been done on dead people.

Crazy Courtroom Queries

Q Were you acquainted with the deceased?

A Yes.

Q Before or after he died?

Q Did you stay all night with this man in London?

A I refuse to answer.

Q Did you stay with him all night in Bristol?

A I refuse to answer.

Q Did you stay all night with him in Dorking?

A No.

Q What can you tell us about the truthfulness and veracity of this defendant?

A Oh, she will tell the truth. She said she'd kill that sonofabitch – and she did!

Q Ms Babler, do you believe that you are emotionally unstable?

A I used to be.

Q How many times have you committed suicide?

A Four times.

As an officer of the Metropolitan Police, did you stop a car bearing the licence number K230 EJK?

 Yes.

 Was the car occupied at the time?

 Where were you on the bike at the time?

 On the seat.

 I meant where on the street were you?

 And lastly Ted, all your answers must be oral, OK?

 Oral.

How old are you?

Oral.

 When was the last time you saw Mr Martin?

 At his funeral.

Did he make any comments to you at that time?

I'm showing you Exhibit 3. Can you say whether you recognize that picture?

That's me.

Were you present when that picture was taken?

Any suggestions as to what prevented this from being a murder trial instead of an attempted murder trial?

The victim lived.

 And what did he do then?

He came home, and next morning he was dead.

So when he woke up the next morning he was dead?

 (Showing man picture.) That's you?

Yes, sir.

Where were you when that picture was taken?

 Do you drink when you're on duty?

I don't drink when I'm on duty, unless I come on duty drunk.

 Are you sexually active?

No, I just lie there.

 Are you qualified to give a urine sample?

I have been since early childhood.

The truth of the matter is that you were not an unbiased, objective witness, isn't it. You too were shot in the fracas?

No, sir. I was shot midway between the fracas and the navel.

What is the meaning of sperm being present?

It indicates intercourse.

Male sperm?

That's the only kind I know.

Can you describe the individual?

He was about medium height and had a beard.

Was this a male or a female?

Could you see him from where you were standing?

I could see his head.

And where was his head?

Just above his shoulders.

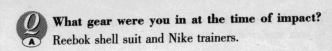

Q **What gear were you in at the time of impact?**
A Reebok shell suit and Nike trainers.

Q **Did he pick the dog up by the ears?**
A No.
Q **What was he doing with the dog's ears?**
A Picking them up in the air.
Q **Where was the dog at this time?**
A Attached to the ears.

Q **Was that the same nose you broke as a child?**
A I have only one, you know.

Q **What happened then?**
A He told me, he says, 'I have to kill you because you can identify me.'
Q **Did he kill you?**
A No.

Officer, what led you to believe the defendant was under the influence?

Because he was argumentary and he couldn't pronunciate his words.

Ms Irving, is your appearance here this morning pursuant to a deposition notice that I sent to your attorney?

No, this is how I dress when I go to work.

Have you lived in this town all your life?

Not yet.

You say you are innocent, yet seven people in this court swore that they saw you steal a watch.

Your honour, I can produce a thousand people who did not see me steal it.

You say the stairs went down to the basement?

Yes.

And these stairs, did they go up also?

Q The youngest son, the 20-year-old, how old is he?

Q Were you alone or by yourself?

Q How long have you been a French-Canadian?

Q Were you present in court this morning when you were sworn in?

Q So you were gone until you returned?

Q Now, you have investigated other murders, have you not, where there was a victim?

Q You don't know what it was, and you don't know what it looked like, but can you describe it?

If you know of any other courtroom howlers send them to the publisher or e-mail them to **jokes@michaelomarabooks.com**

Stupid Laws
of Europe

Denmark

■ Before starting a car the driver must check the lights, brakes, steering and sound the horn. A visual check is also necessary to ensure there are no children hidden underneath the car.

■ If a horse carriage is trying to pass a car and the horse becomes unsettled, the driver is legally required to pull over and stop. If the horse becomes increasingly agitated and has to be calmed down, the driver has to cover up the car by law.

■ It is not a crime to attempt to escape from prison, but if an escapee is later caught, he/she has to finish the remainder of his/her sentence.

■ No one may start a car while someone is underneath the vehicle.

■ Headlights must be switched on *whenever* a vehicle is being driven in order to distinguish it from parked cars.

■ When driving, there must be another person in front of the car waving a flag to warn horse-drawn carriages that a motor car is approaching.

Did you know?
In London it is against the law to fall asleep on a bus; a London bus company recently prosecuted a nun whose ticket had become invalid after she fell asleep and missed her stop.

England

- The impersonation of Chelsea Pensioners is illegal.

- It is unlawful to be drunk on licensed premises e.g. in a pub or bar.

- Until recently it was against the law to sell most goods on Sunday, though it has always been acceptable to sell carrots on the Sabbath.

- It is a crime for two adult men to have sex in the same house as a third person.

- Beds must not be hung out of windows.

- It is forbidden for a lady to eat chocolates on public transport.

- It is against the law to eat mince pies on 25 December.

- Any boy under the age of ten is not allowed to see a naked shop dummy.

- It is not legal for a Member of Parliament to enter the House of Commons wearing a full suit of armour.

- All Englishmen over 14 years old are meant to carry out about two hours of longbow practice a week under the supervision of the local clergy.

- A man is allowed to urinate in public, as long as it is on the rear wheel of his car and his right hand is on the vehicle.

- Committing suicide is classified as a capital crime (repealed).

CITY LAWS

CHESTER

■ A Welsh person may be shot with a bow and arrow as long as the event occurs within the city walls and after midnight.

HEREFORD

■ You can shoot a Welsh person all day, but only on Sundays, with a longbow, in the Cathedral Close.

LONDON

■ You are acknowledged as a freeman if you can drive your geese down Cheapside.

■ London Hackney carriages (taxicabs) must carry a bale of hay and a sack of oats by law.

■ Since the seventeenth century it has been illegal for a man to hit his wife after 9 p.m.

YORK

■ Upon sight of a Scotsman, it is perfectly legal to shoot him with a bow and arrow, except on Sundays.

■ Any Scotsman caught farting on a Sunday can be shot with a bow and arrow.

Legal Laughs I

It was so cold in Montana that the lawyers
had their hands in their own pockets.

∾

How many lawyers does it take to shingle a roof?

3½ if you slice 'em right.

∾

What is the difference between a
female lawyer and a bulldog?

Lipstick!

∾

Did you hear they just released a new Barbie doll
called 'Divorced Barbie'?

Yeah, it comes with all of Ken's stuff.

∾

What do you call a bus-load of lawyers
at the bottom of the ocean?

A good start.

∾

What do you call a smiling, sober, courteous
person at a Bar Association convention?

The caterer.

France

■ Kissing on French railways is forbidden.

■ It is illegal to park or land a flying saucer in any vineyard across France.

■ Between the hours of 8 a.m. and 8 p.m., 70% of the music played on the radio must be by French composers.

■ It is a crime for an owner of a pig to call his swine 'Napoleon'.

CITY LAWS

ANTIBES

■ It is against the law to take photographs of police officers or police vehicles, even if they are just in the background.

Greece

■ If a man is caught kissing a woman in public the death penalty may be enforced.

Holland

- It is illegal to sell beer and wine on Sunday, but mixed drinks are available by the glass.

- Prostitution is legal but the prostitutes must pay taxes like any other business.

- In one Dutch region it is a crime to breach the dykes of a river, even though the region has no rivers.

- It is semi-legal to smoke pot.

Iceland

- It is permissible for anyone to practice medicine as long as he/she displays a sign that reads *Scottulaejnir*, which translates as 'quack doctor'.

Ireland

- Any person who shall pretend or exercise to use any type of witchcraft, sorcery, enchantment, or pretend knowledge in any occult or craft or science shall for any such offence suffer imprisonment at the time of one whole year and also shall be obliged to obscursion for his/her good behaviour (1736).

Legal Laughs II

What's the problem with lawyer jokes?

Lawyers don't think they're funny and no one else thinks they're jokes.

∽

How many lawyers does it take to change a light bulb?

None if they still have a secretary.

∽

What's the difference between a lawyer and a catfish?

One is a slimy, bottom-dwelling, scum-sucker. The other is a fish.

∽

How many lawyer jokes are there?

Just two, all the rest are true.

∽

Why are lawyers like nuclear weapons?

If one side has one, the other side has to get one; once launched, they can't be recalled; and when they land, they screw everything up for the next 20 years.

Italy

- A man may be arrested for wearing a skirt.

- It is illegal to swear in public.

- Under an Italian code of criminal law, it is possible to be charged with six-month prison sentences for insulting public officials.

- It is against the law to be a professional charlatan.

- Striking someone with a fist is considered a crime.

- According to local law women christened Mary are not allowed to work as prostitutes.

Norway

- In accordance with the law, female dogs or cats must not be spayed, though it is quite permissible to neuter the males of the species.

Scotland

- Fishing is not permitted on Sundays.

- It is against the law to be drunk in possession of a cow.

- Trespassing on someone else's land is legal.

- You are presumed guilty until proven innocent for certain misdemeanours.

- If someone knocks on your door and requires the use of your commode, you are obliged by law to allow them entry.

Switzerland

- Clothes may not be hung out to dry on Sundays.

- Cars must not be washed on a Sunday.

- It is considered an offence to mow the lawn on a Sunday, because of the noise pollution it may cause.

- It is against the law to flush the toilet after 10 p.m. if you live in an apartment.

- A man may not relieve himself while standing up, after 10 p.m.

- Though it is illegal to produce, store, sell and trade absinthe, it is perfectly legal to consume it.

- Every car with snow tyres must have a sticker on its dashboard stating that the driver should not drive faster than 160 km/h (100 m.p.h.) with these tyres.

- If you leave your car-keys inside your car and leave the car doors unlocked, you will be punished.

Legal Laughs III

How many personal injury attorneys
does it take to change a light bulb?

**Three – one to turn the bulb, one to
shake him off the ladder and the
third to sue the ladder company.**

∽∾∽

What do you get when you cross the
Godfather with a lawyer?

An offer you can't understand.

∽∾∽

What is a criminal lawyer?

Redundant.

∽∾∽

How do you save a drowning lawyer?

Take your foot off his head.

∽∾∽

What's black and brown and looks good
on an attorney?

A Doberman pinscher.

Stupid Laws
of Australasia

Australia

- Children are not allowed to buy cigarettes, but it is quite legal for them to smoke cigarettes.

- It is against the law to leave one's car keys in an unattended vehicle.

- Reading someone's tarot or giving someone a psychic reading is illegal, as these are forms of witchcraft.

- By law, taxicabs must carry a bale of hay in the boot.

- Bars are required to stable, water and feed the horses of their customers.

- The legal age for straight sex is 16 years, unless the person is in the care/custody of the older person, in which case it is 18 years.

- Sex with a kangaroo is only permissible when drunk.

- In some states it is against the law to own certain types of mattress without a mattress licence.

Tasmania

STATE LAWS

■ Until the tragic massacre in Port Arthur it was legal to own an AK-47 but not legal to be gay.

Victoria

STATE LAWS

■ It is an offence to wear pink hot pants after midday on Sundays.

■ Only licensed electricians are permitted to change a light bulb. If this law is broken a $10 fine is charged.

■ Women must wear a neck-to-knee swimsuit in order to swim at Brighton Beach; anything more revealing is against the law.

Did you know?
In some parts of Australia, urinating in a public place is not permitted, but if the act is performed by a man and directed against the rear, kerbside wheel of a motor vehicle it is quite legal.

Stupid Laws of Asia

China

- A maximum of one child is allowed per household; if a second child is born, a fine may be charged.

- It is against the law to save a drowning person, as such an act would interfere with his or her fate.

- A student has to be intelligent to be allowed to attend college.

CITY LAWS

BEIJING

- Under Beijing traffic laws, drivers of power-driven vehicles who stop at pedestrian crossings may be given a warning and could be fined up to 5 yuan.

Legal Laughs IV

What's the difference between a
lawyer and a trampoline?

**You take off your shoes before
you jump on a trampoline.**

❦

What do you have when a lawyer is buried up
to his neck in wet cement?

Not enough cement.

❦

Why does California have the most
attorneys, and New Jersey have the
most toxic waste dumps?

New Jersey got first pick.

❦

How do you get a lawyer out
of a tree?

Cut the rope.

❦

JURY: A collection of people banded together for
the purpose of deciding which side has hired the
better lawyer.

India

■ It is against the law to leave *more* than five rat's hairs or droppings for every kilo of rice, wheat, maize or food grain.

> **Did you know?**
> *An elephant was recently prosecuted for manslaughter in New Delhi after she trampled a man to death. Police refused to release the 44-year-old pachyderm until the judge hearing the case granted bail.*

Indonesia

■ The penalty for masturbation is decapitation.

Israel

- It is unlawful to ride a bicycle without a licence.

- It is forbidden to raise a pig on Israeli soil. If this law is broken the punishment is to kill the pig.

- If an illegal radio station has been running for five years or more, the station becomes legal.

CITY LAWS

ARAD

- The feeding of animals in public places is prohibited.

- It is considered an offence to operate a mobile spay/neuter clinic as it constitutes peddling.

KIRIAT MOTZKIN

- No loud voices or big lights are allowed during weekends.

RAMAT-HASHARON

- It is forbidden to raise Rottweiler dogs.

Japan

- There is no age of consent.

Lebanon

- Men are legally allowed to have sex with animals, but the animals must be female. Having sexual relations with a male animal is punishable by death.

Saudi Arabia

- It is illegal to kiss a stranger.

- Male doctors are not allowed to examine women.

- Women doctors are forbidden.

- It is considered an offence if a woman appears in public, unless she is accompanied by a male relative or guardian.

- A woman is not permitted to drive a car.

Legal Laughs V

A lawyer named 'Strange' was shopping for a tombstone. After he had made his selection, the stonecutter asked him what inscription he would like on it.

'Here lies an honest man and a lawyer,' responded the lawyer.

'Sorry, but I can't do that,' replied the stonecutter. 'In this state, it's against the law to bury two people in the same grave. However, I could put *"Here lies an honest lawyer".'*

'But that won't let people know who it is,' protested the lawyer.

'It most certainly will,' retorted the stonecutter. 'People will read it and exclaim, "That's Strange!"'

∽∾∽

When questioning potential jurors for an upcoming trial the judge inquired, 'Is there any reason why any of you cannot see this trial through to its conclusion?'

A lone juror spoke up. 'I can't!' stated the woman.

'Why, just looking at the woman I'm convinced she's guilty!'

'Madam,' said the judge. 'That's the prosecutor.'

Singapore

■ It is illegal to eat chewing gum on subways. If anyone is caught breaking this law they may face a fine, jail or even both.

■ The sale of chewing gum is forbidden.

■ Homosexuals are banned from living in the country.

■ Oral sex is a crime unless it is used as a form of foreplay.

■ Pornography is illegal.

■ Citizens must not walk around naked while in their homes as such activity is classed as pornography.

■ After using a public toilet, you are legally obliged to flush. A fine of 200–1000 Singapore dollars may be imposed on those who forget to flush.

■ It is a crime to cross the street within 50 metres of a pedestrian crossing. At 50 metres or more it is legal.

■ If convicted of dropping litter three times, the law-breaker has to clean the streets on Sundays wearing a sign saying, 'I am a litterer'. This punishment will then be broadcast on the local news.

■ It is illegal to pee in a lift.

South Korea

- Traffic police must report all bribes that they receive from motorists.

Thailand

- Leaving the house without wearing underwear is a crime.

- A shirt must be worn while driving a car.

- You must pay a fine of $600 if you are caught throwing away chewed bubble gum on the pavement. If you do not pay the fine, you are jailed.

- It is an offence to step on any of the nation's currency.

Stupid Laws of
North America

Canada

■ It is an offence to graze a llama in a National Park; law-breakers may be subject to a $75 fine.

■ Every fifth song on Canadian radio must be by a Canadian-born citizen, which means Celine Dion and Bryan Adams get played very often.

■ Boarding a plane while it is in flight is illegal.

■ It is against the law to pay for a fifty-cent item using only pennies.

■ It is illegal to launch a missile in an undesignated area; those who break this law may be punished with a $75 fine.

■ The removal of bandages in public is not permitted.

■ Mounties always get their man.

■ Anyone guilty of hindering Canadian forces while marching may face a fine of $300.

Alberta

PROVINCIAL LAWS

- Businesses are legally obliged to provide rails for tying up horses.

- Wooden logs must not be painted.

- It is against the law to use dice to play craps.

- After release from prison, it is required by law that an ex-prisoner is provided with a handgun with bullets and a horse, so he/she can ride out of town.

CITY LAWS

CALGARY

- It is against the law to set off firecrackers or throw snowballs without permission from the mayor or City Council.

EDMONTON

- It is illegal for a man to drink with a woman in a beer parlour.

- All cyclists must signal with their arm before making a turn, though they must also keep both hands on the handlebars at all times.

British Columbia

PROVINCIAL LAWS

- It is an offence to kill a sasquatch.

- Anyone interrupting a meeting of the British Columbia Grasshopper Control Committee is committing a crime and may be arrested.

Manitoba

CITY LAWS

WINNIPEG

- It is unlawful to be naked in your own home if the blinds are left up.

- It is an offence to strike the pavement with a metal object.

Legal Laughs VI

Firemen and paramedics were working frantically to remove an attorney from his demolished car which was just involved in a head-on collision.

'Oh ... my Mercedes, my poor Mercedes ... Oh ...' the attorney kept repeating through his pain.

'Look fella,' said the paramedic, 'quit worrying so much about your car. Your entire arm has been severed below the elbow and you could bleed to death!'

As the attorney looks down to see his arm missing, he begins whimpering, 'My Rolex, my poor Rolex ... Oh ...'

An attorney ran over to the office of his client.

'I can't believe it!' said the angered attorney. 'You sent a case of Dom Perignon to the judge in your case? That judge is as straight as an arrow. Now we're certain to lose this case!'

'Relax,' said the client, 'I sent it in the prosecutor's name.'

New Brunswick

PROVINCIAL LAWS

■ Driving on the roads is prohibited.

Nova Scotia

PROVINCIAL LAWS

■ A person is not allowed to water his/her lawn when it is raining.

■ Lighting a fart while smoking carries a $100 fine.

CITY LAWS

HALIFAX

■ No citizen is allowed to chop wood on the pavement.

Ontario

PROVINCIAL LAWS

■ The speed limit is 80 km/h for cars, but cyclists have the right of way.

CITY LAWS

COBOURG

■ If you have a water trough in your front yard it is unlawful to fill it any later than 5 a.m.

ETOBICOKE

■ It is an offence to fill a bath with more than 3.5 inches of water.

GUELPH

■ The city is classified as a 'no-pee' zone.

KANATA

■ The colour of house and garage doors is regulated by city by-laws; you can be fined if you paint your door purple.

■ Citizens are not allowed to make repairs to their car(s) in the street.

OSHAWA

■ It is a crime to climb trees.

■ Homeowners are responsible for clearing snow from municipal pavements. If the pavement is not cleaned within 24 hours after a snowfall, city workers will clear it up and the cost will be added to the homeowners' tax bill.

OTTAWA

- It is against the law to eat ice cream on Bank Street on a Sunday.

- Children are not allowed to eat ice-cream cones on the streets on the Sabbath.

TORONTO

- It is unlawful to drag a dead horse down Yonge Street on a Sunday.

- Cinema owners are forbidden to start a film that will end after 2 a.m.

- Residents are not allowed to saw wood or wash their cars on the street.

UXBRIDGE

- Residents are not allowed to have an Internet connection faster than 56k.

WAWA

- Local residents must not paint ladders because if the steps are wet, they become slippery and dangerous, and an accident could result.

- It is illegal to be affectionate in public on Sundays.

WINDSOR

- It is an offence to play a musical instrument in the park.

Quebec

PROVINCIAL LAWS

■ All business signs must be in French. If the business operator wishes to have English on the sign, it must be at least half the size of the French. There are no laws restricting the usage of other languages on signs.

■ No language other than French can be shown out of doors.

CITY LAWS

BEACONSFIELD

■ It is considered an offence to have more than two colours of paint on your house.

■ It is against the law to own a log cabin.

MONTREAL

■ The Queen Elizabeth Hotel must feed your horse without charge when you rent a room.

■ It is an offence to park one's car in such a way that it is blocking one's own driveway.

■ 'For sale' signs are not allowed in the windows of moving vehicles.

- Cars parked in public places must be locked, and their windows must be wound down to less than the width of a hand.

- The rear numberplate of a vehicle must not be protected by glass or plastic.

- People are not permitted to swear in French.

- Citizens must not relieve themselves or spit on the street. This crime is punishable by a fine of at least $100.

OUTREMONT

- It is illegal to leave your horse in front of the Country Squire (local hotel) without fastening it securely to the hitching post – which was removed years ago.

Saskatchewan

CITY LAWS

FORT QU'APPELLE

- Teenagers must not walk down the main street with their shoelaces untied.

SASKATOON

- It is an offence to try and catch fish with one's hands.

Legal Laughs VII

A man walking along the beach one day found a bottle. He rubbed it and, sure enough, out popped a genie.

'I will grant you three wishes,' said the genie. 'But there is a catch.'

'What catch?' the man asked.

The genie replied, 'Every time you make a wish, every lawyer in the world will receive double the wish you were granted.'

'Well, I can live with that! No problem!' replied the elated man.

'What is your first wish?' asked the genie.

'Well, I've always wanted a Ferrari!'

POOF! A Ferrari appeared in front of the man.

'Now every lawyer in the world has two Ferraris,' said the genie. 'Next wish?'

'I'd love a million pounds,' replied the man.

POOF! One million pounds appeared at his feet.

'Now every lawyer in the world has two million pounds,' said the genie.

'Well, that's okay, as long as I've got my million,' replied the man.

'What is your third and final wish?'

The man thought long and hard, and finally said,

'Well, you know, I've always wanted to donate a kidney...'

USA

Did you know?
Sending an entire building by post has been illegal in the US since 1916, when a man mailed a 40,000 tonne brick house across Utah to avoid high freight rates.

Alabama

STATE LAWS

- It is against the law for a driver to wear a blindfold when operating a vehicle.

- Dominoes must not be played on Sunday.

- Driving a motorboat on city streets is an offence.

- It is illegal to wear a false moustache that causes inappropriate laughter in church.

- Sprinkling salt on a railroad track may be punishable by death.

- It is not permissible to flick snot into the wind.

- You must not carry an ice-cream cone in your back pocket at any time.

- Pigeons are prohibited from eating pebbles from composite roofs.

- It is a crime to wear a mask in public.

CITY LAWS

LEE COUNTY

■ It is illegal to sell peanuts after sunset on a Wednesday.

> **Did you know?**
> *In an attempt to cut down on the number of laws that govern them, the residents of Brooksville, Alabama, applied to be governed by no other law than the Ten Commandments.*

Alaska

STATE LAWS

■ It is against the law to look at moose from an aeroplane.

■ It is considered a crime to push a live moose out of a moving aeroplane.

CITY LAWS

FAIRBANKS

■ It is unlawful to give alcoholic beverages to a moose.

Arizona

STATE LAWS

- Donkeys are not allowed to sleep in bathtubs.
- You may not have more than two dildos in a house.
- It is against the law to hunt camels.

CITY LAWS

GLOBE

- It is unlawful to play cards in the street with a Native American.

MARICOPA COUNTY

- No more than six girls may live in any house.

NOGALES

- An ordinance prohibits the wearing of suspenders.
- No one is permitted to ride their horse up the stairs of the county courthouse.

TUCSON

- Women are not allowed to wear trousers.

Arkansas

STATE LAWS

- A law provides that schoolteachers who bob their hair will not get a rise.
- Oral sex is considered to be sodomy.
- It is an offence to keep alligators in bathtubs.

CITY LAWS

LITTLE ROCK

- It is illegal to mispronounce the name of the state of Arkansas.
- Men and women who flirt in the street may face a 30-day jail sentence.
- It is unlawful to walk one's cow down Main Street after 1 p.m. on Sunday.
- Dogs are not allowed to bark after 6 p.m.

California

STATE LAWS

- Women may not drive wearing a housecoat.

- Ownership of a gerbil, hamster or ferret is illegal.

- It's a crime to set up a mousetrap without a hunting licence.

- Legally, no one has the right to try and stop a child from jumping over puddles of water.

- It is against the law to peel an orange in a hotel room.

- Animals are banned from mating publicly within 1500 feet of a tavern, school, or place of worship.

- The shooting of game from a moving vehicle is an offence, unless the target is a whale.

CITY LAWS

ARCADIA

- Peacocks have right of way when crossing any street, including driveways.

BALDWIN PARK

- Bicycles must not be ridden in swimming pools.

BELVEDERE

■ A City Council order advises that 'no dog shall be in a public place without its master on a lead'.

BERKELEY

■ It's a crime to whistle for your lost canary before 7 a.m.

BLYTHE

■ A city ordinance declares that a person must own at least two cows before he is allowed to wear cowboy boots.

CARMEL

■ Women are not allowed to wear high heels within the city limits.

CHICO

■ Detonating a nuclear device within the city limits results in a $500 fine.

GLENDALE

■ Horror films can only be shown on Mondays, Tuesdays or Wednesdays.

HOLLYWOOD

■ It is illegal to drive more than two thousand sheep down Hollywood Boulevard at one time.

LONG BEACH

■ Only cars can be stored in a garage; no other items are permitted.

■ It is illegal to swear on a mini-golf course.

LOS ANGELES

■ You cannot bathe two babies in the same bathtub at the same time.

■ Crying on the witness stand is not allowed.

■ Toads must not be licked. The toad secretes a poison that some people lick to get high.

■ You cannot poke a turkey to see how tender it is.

■ A man is legally entitled to beat his wife with a leather belt or strap, but the belt can't be wider than two inches, unless he has his wife's consent to beat her with a wider strap.

■ It is an offence to possess a hippopotamus.

■ The hunting of moths under streetlights is forbidden.

ONTARIO

■ It is illegal for roosters to crow within the city limits.

PASADENA

■ It is unlawful for a secretary to be alone in a room with her boss.

RIVERSIDE

■ People must not carry their lunches down the street between 11 a.m. and 1 a.m.

SAN FRANCISCO

■ Elephants are not allowed to stroll down Market Street unless they are on a lead.

■ It is illegal to wipe one's car with underwear.

■ Persons classified as 'ugly' are not permitted to walk down any street.

■ Oral sex is prohibited, whether given or received.

Legal Laughs VIII

After an electrician finished repairing some faulty wiring in a lawyer's home he handed him the bill.

'Four hundred pounds! For an hour's work?' cried the lawyer. 'That's ridiculous! Why I'm a lawyer and I don't charge that much.'

To which the electrician replied, 'Funny, when I was a lawyer I didn't either!'

༺༒༻

A priest settled into a chair in a lawyer's office.

'Is it true,' said the priest, 'that your firm does not charge members of the clergy?'

'I'm afraid you're misinformed,' stated the lawyer. 'People in your profession can look forward to a reward in the next world, but we lawyers have to take ours in this one.'

༺༒༻

A man walked into a bar with an alligator.

'Do you serve lawyers in here?' the man enquired.

'Sure do!' replied the bartender.

'Great!' the man said. 'I'll have a beer, and how 'bout a lawyer for my 'gator.'

Colorado

STATE LAWS

■ At a marriage service it is an offence to throw shoes at the bride and groom.

CITY LAWS

DENVER

■ It is unlawful to lend your vacuum cleaner to your next-door neighbour.

■ Black cars must not be driven on Sundays.

LOGAN COUNTY

■ A man is not allowed to kiss a woman while she is asleep.

PUEBLO

■ Growing dandelions within the city limits is against the law.

STERLING

■ Cats may only run loose if they have been fitted with a taillight.

Connecticut

STATE LAWS

- You cannot be stopped by the police for biking over 65 m.p.h.

- Pedestrians are not allowed to walk across a street on their hands.

- In order for a pickle to be officially classed as a pickle it must bounce.

CITY LAWS

DEVON

- It is unlawful to walk backwards after sunset.

HARTFORD

- Men are not allowed to kiss their wives on Sundays.

WATERBURY

- Beauticians are forbidden from humming, singing or whistling when working on a customer.

Legal Laughs IX

A Dublin lawyer died in poverty and many barristers of the city subscribed to a fund for his funeral. The Lord Chief Justice of Orbury was asked to donate a shilling.

'Only a shilling to bury an attorney?' said the Justice. 'Here's a guinea, go and bury 20 of them.'

❧

Two lawyers were walking along negotiating a case.

'Look,' said one, 'let's be honest with each other.'

'Okay, you first,' replied the other.

That was the end of the discussion.

❧

Humpty Dumpty, the tooth fairy, an ol' drunk and an honest attorney are all walking down the street together. Simultaneously, they each spot a £50-note lying on the pavement. Who gets the money? Answer: The ol' drunk, of course. The other three individuals only exist in fairy tales.

Delaware

STATE LAWS

■ It is illegal to fly over any body of water, unless there is enough food and drink aboard the aircraft.

■ It is an offence to try to pawn one's wooden leg.

CITY LAWS

LEWES

■ Getting married for a dare legally entitles the couple to an annulment.

Florida

STATE LAWS

- A woman may be fined for falling asleep under a hair dryer, as can the salon owner.

- Men may not be seen wearing any kind of strapless gown in public.

- Conducting sexual relations with a porcupine is unlawful.

- When having sex, only the missionary position is legal.

- It is against the law to break wind in a public place after 6 p.m. on Thursdays.

- It is considered an offence to shower naked.

- A husband must not kiss his wife's breasts.

- Unmarried women are prohibited from parachuting on Sundays; otherwise they risk arrest, fine, and/or jailing.

- If an elephant is left tied to a parking meter, the parking fee has to be paid just as it would for a vehicle.

- It is illegal to sing in a public place while wearing a swimsuit.

- Housewives are forbidden from breaking more than three dishes in one day or chipping the edges of more than four cups and/or saucers.

- It is unlawful to hunt or kill deer while swimming.

CITY LAWS

DAYTONA BEACH

■ Rubbish bins must not be molested.

KEY WEST

■ An ordinance exists to prohibit turtle racing within the city limits.

TAMPA BAY

■ It is illegal to eat cottage cheese on Sunday after 6 p.m.

Georgia

STATE LAWS

■ It is a crime to swear in front of a dead body that is lying in a coroner's office or funeral home.

■ When citizens attend church worship on a Sunday they must be equipped with a loaded rifle.

CITY LAWS

ACWORTH

■ All citizens must own a rake by law.

ATLANTA

■ It is against the law to tie a giraffe to a telephone pole or street lamp.

COLUMBUS

■ It is an offence to cut off a chicken's head on a Sunday.

■ It is a crime to carry a chicken by its feet down Broadway on Sunday.

MARIETTA

■ It is illegal to spit from a car or a bus, but citizens are allowed to spit from a truck.

QUITMAN

■ Chickens are prohibited from crossing the road within the city limits.

Legal Laughs X

A lawyer's dog, running about off his lead, headed straight for the local butcher's shop and stole a roast off the counter. The butcher went to the lawyer's office and asked, 'If a dog steals a piece of meat from my store, do I have a right to demand payment for the meat from the dog's owner?'

'Absolutely,' the lawyer responded.

The butcher immediately shot back, 'Good! You owe me £7.99 for the roast your dog stole from me this morning.'

The lawyer, without a word, wrote the butcher a cheque for £7.99. A few days later, the butcher, browsing through his mail, found an envelope from the lawyer. The contents read 'Consultation: £25.00.'

⚬⚬⚬

A millionaire informed his attorney, 'I want a stipulation in my will that my wife is to inherit everything, but only if she remarries within six months of my death.'

'Why such an odd stipulation?' asked the attorney.

'Because I want someone to be sorry I died!' came the reply.

Hawaii

STATE LAWS

■ Fines can be inflicted upon locals who do not own a boat.

■ Citizens are not allowed to put coins in their ears.

■ It is illegal to say, 'Book 'em Danno'.

IDAHO

STATE LAWS

■ It is considered an offence to ride on a merry-go-round on Sundays.

■ It is illegal for a man to give his sweetheart a box of sweets/chocolates weighing less than 50lbs.

■ People are not allowed to participate in dog fights.

BOISE

■ Residents may not fish from a giraffe's back.

COEUR D'ALENE

■ Any officer who suspects that sex is taking place in a car must drive up from behind, sound his horn or flash his lights three times and wait approximately two minutes before getting out of his car to investigate.

POCATELLO

■ A person may not be seen in public without a smile on their face.

Illinois

STATE LAWS

- It is against the law to speak English.
- You must contact the police before entering the city in an automobile.
- All bachelors must be called master, not mister, when addressed by their female counterparts.
- A law requires all healthy men aged 21–50 years to work in the streets for two days per year.

CITY LAWS

CHAMPAIGN

- It is considered an offence to urinate in your neighbour's mouth.

Did you know?
On the Chicago breakwater it is a crime to fish in pyjamas.

CHICAGO

■ It is against the law to eat in an establishment that is on fire.

■ It is unlawful to give a dog whisky to drink.

■ It is legal to protest naked in front of city hall as long as you are under 17 years old and possess a relevant permit.

■ Animals can go to jail. A monkey served five days in a Chicago jail for shoplifting.

CICERO

■ Humming on public streets on Sundays is prohibited.

CRETE

■ It is considered a crime to attempt to have sex with one's dog.

EUREKA

■ Men with a moustache may not kiss women.

GALESBURG

■ There is a $1000 fine imposed for beating rats with baseball bats.

JOLIET

■ A woman can get arrested for trying on more than six dresses in one store.

KENILWORTH

■ Roosters must retreat 300 feet from any residence if they wish to crow. Hens that wish to cackle must retreat 200 feet.

KIRKLAND

■ Bees are forbidden from flying over or through any of its streets.

MOLINE

■ During the summer months of June and August, ice skating at the riverside pond is forbidden.

OBLONG

■ It's punishable by law to make love while hunting or fishing on your wedding day.

URBANA

■ It is against the law for a monster to enter the city limits.

WINNETKA

■ Theatre managers can kick out any patron who has 'odoriferous feet'.

ZION

■ It is a crime for anyone to give lighted cigars to dogs, cats or any other domesticated animals kept as pets.

Indiana

STATE LAWS

- It is against the law to shoot open a can of food.

- Men who are always kissing others are not allowed to grow moustaches.

- Bathing is prohibited during the winter.

- Known as 3.1415 in the rest of the world, Pi is known as 4 in Indiana.

- Citizens are not allowed to go to a cinema or theatre, or ride on a tram within at least four hours after eating garlic.

CITY LAWS

BEECH GROVE

- It is forbidden to eat watermelon in the park.

FRENCH LICK SPRINGS

- All black cats must wear bells on Friday 13th.

SOUTH BEND

- It is illegal for a monkey to smoke cigarettes.

Iowa

STATE LAWS

- Kisses may last for a maximum of five minutes.

- One-armed piano players are required by law to perform for free.

- A man with a moustache may never kiss a woman in public.

- A man isn't allowed more than three gulps of beer while lying in bed with a woman or holding a woman in his arms.

CITY LAWS

FORT MADISON

- Fire-fighters must practice dealing with a fire for 15 minutes before answering an emergency call.

MARSHALLTOWN

- Horses are not allowed to eat fire hydrants.

OTTUMWA

- It is unlawful for any male person within the corporate limits of the city to wink at any female person with whom he is unacquainted.

Kansas

STATE LAWS

- It is illegal for chicken thieves to work during the daytime.

- Catching fish with one's bare hands is against the law.

- The state game rule forbids the use of mules in the hunting of ducks.

CITY LAWS

McLOUGH

- It is illegal to wash one's false teeth in a public drinking fountain.

NATOMA

- It's against the law to practise knife-throwing at men wearing striped suits.

RUSSELL

- It is against the law to have a musical car horn.

WICHITA

- A father cannot frighten his daughter's boyfriend with a gun.

Kentucky

STATE LAWS

■ It is illegal to utter profanities when talking about country music singer Loretta Lynn.

■ By law, anyone who has been drinking is 'sober' until he or she 'cannot hold on to the ground'.

■ Any female between the weight of 90–200 lbs appearing in a bathing suit on a highway must be escorted by at least two officers or armed with a club. The law does not apply to anyone weighing less or more than 90–200 lbs.

■ A woman can not remarry the same man more than four times.

■ Every person must take a bath at least once a year.

■ It is against the law to use a reptile during any part of a religious service.

CITY LAWS

FRANKFORT

■ It is against the law to shoot a policeman's tie.

LEXINGTON

■ It is illegal to transport an ice-cream cone in your pocket.

OWENSBORO

■ It is a crime for any woman to buy a hat without her husband's approval.

■ Anyone who receives anal sex is breaking the law.

Louisiana

STATE LAWS

■ There are no state height restrictions, so citizens can grow as tall as they please.

■ It is against the law to rob a bank and then shoot at the cashier with a water pistol.

■ Biting someone with your natural teeth is classed as 'simple assault', while biting someone with false teeth is classified as 'aggravated assault'.

■ It is a crime to gargle in public places.

Did you know?
Under legislation passed recently, children from kindergarten to high school in Louisiana must address their teachers and other employees as 'Sir' or 'Ma'am' or use Mr, Mrs, Miss or Ms. They have been banned from talking to teachers like Bart Simpson.

CITY LAWS

LAKE CHARLES

■ It is an offence for a rain puddle to remain on a front lawn for more than twelve hours.

NEW ORLEANS

■ Alligators must not be tied to fire hydrants.

Maine

STATE LAWS

- Passengers are forbidden from stepping out of a plane in flight.

- It's against the law to molest an alligator.

- There is a law that calls for a legal hunting season on all attorneys.

- If Christmas decorations are still kept up after 14 January, householders are liable to be fined.

CITY LAWS

AUGUSTA

- Strolling down the street playing a violin is against the law.

PORTLAND

- Shoelaces must be tied while walking down the street.

- It is against the law for a wedding ceremony to be performed at a skating rink.

- It is illegal to tickle a girl under the chin with a feather duster.

RUMFORD

- It is forbidden for tenants to bite their landlords.

Maryland

STATE LAWS

- Thistles may not grow in one's yard.

- It is illegal to sell condoms from vending machines except 'in places where alcoholic beverages are sold for consumption on the premises'.

CITY LAWS

BALTIMORE

- It's a crime to throw bales of hay from a second-storey window within the city limits.

- Lions must not be taken to the cinema.

- It is an offence to mistreat oysters.

OCEAN CITY

- Eating while swimming in the ocean is prohibited.

Massachusetts

STATE LAWS

■ Mourners at a wake may not eat more than three sandwiches.

■ Snoring is forbidden by law unless all bedroom windows are closed and securely locked.

■ It is illegal to go to bed without having a proper bath first.

■ A woman cannot be on top in sexual activities.

■ Gorillas are not allowed in the back seat of any car.

■ Quakers and witches are banned.

■ It is against the law to use bullets as currency.

■ An old ordinance declares goatees illegal unless you first pay a special licence fee for the privilege of wearing one in public.

■ Taxi drivers are prohibited from making love in the front seat of their taxi during their shifts.

■ During the month of April, all dogs must have their hind legs tied.

CITY LAWS

BOSTON

- Two people are not allowed to kiss in front of a church.

- It is illegal to take a bath unless one has been ordered to by a physician.

- It is forbidden to take baths on a Sunday.

- All public displays of affection are forbidden on Sundays.

- Pedestrians always have right of way.

- Anyone may let their sheep and cows graze in the public gardens/commons at any time except on Sundays.

- Eating peanuts in church is prohibited.

LONGMEADOW

- It is illegal for two men to carry a bathtub across the town green.

MARLBOROUGH

- Nuclear devices must not be detonated.
- A citizen is allowed to own a maximum of two dogs.

Michigan

STATE LAWS

- A man legally owns his wife's hair, and so a woman isn't allowed to have her hair cut without her husband's permission.

- There is a ten-cent bounty for each rat's head brought into a town office.

- It is legal for a robber to file a lawsuit if he/she got hurt whilst burgling your house.

- A farmer is legally entitled to sleep with his pigs, cows, horses, goats and chickens.

- It is a crime to place a skunk under your boss's desk.

CITY LAWS

GRAND HAVEN

- If a person throws an abandoned hoop skirt into any street or on to any pavement, he/she can be fined $5 for committing such an offence.

DETROIT

- It is illegal for a man to scowl at his wife on Sundays.

- Couples are not allowed to make love in their cars generally, unless the vehicle is parked on their own property.

Minnesota

STATE LAWS

- If a person stands in front of a moving train, he/she is breaking the law and may be jailed.

- No man is allowed to make love to his wife with the smell of garlic, onions or sardines on his breath. If his wife so requests, law mandates that he must brush his teeth.

- It is against the law to hang men and women's underwear on the same clothesline.

- It is a crime to sleep in the nude.

CITY LAWS

MINNEAPOLIS

- Anyone guilty of double-parking a car will be put on a chain-gang and fed only bread and water.

ROCHESTER

- All bathing suits have to be inspected by the head of police.

Did you know?
Under legislation to protect transvestites from discrimination, a male transvestite teacher from Minnesota was granted permission to use the female toilets with the schoolgirls.

Mississippi

CITY LAWS

CANTON

■ It is a crime to kill a squirrel with a gun in a courtroom.

COLUMBUS

■ The fine for waving a gun in public is higher than actually shooting it.

MERIDIAN

■ Rolling a safe down the street on its wheels is forbidden.

OXFORD

■ Driving around the square more than 100 times in a single session is illegal.

TYLERTOWN

■ It is against the law to shave in the centre of Main Street.

Legal Laughs XI

George and Harry set out in a trans-Atlantic hot-air balloon race. After 37 hours in the air and appearing lost, George said, 'We'd better lose some altitude so we can see exactly where we are.' Hesitantly, Harry let some hot air out of the balloon, and it began to descend slowly below the cloud cover. Still confused as to their exact location George again said, 'I still can't tell where we are Harry. Let's ask that gentleman down there on the ground.'

Harry yelled down to the stranger, 'Excuse me mate, can you tell us where we are?'

'You're in a balloon about 100 feet up in the air,' came the reply.

'That man must be a lawyer,' George quipped.

'How can you tell?' asked Harry.

'Because the advice he just gave us is 100% accurate and totally useless!'

~⚬~

'You seem to have more than the average share of intelligence for a man of your background,' sneered the lawyer at a witness on the stand.

'If I wasn't under oath, I'd return the compliment,' replied the witness.

Missouri

STATE LAWS

■ Any city can levy a tax to support a band, as long as the mayor plays piccolo and each band member can eat peas with a knife.

CITY LAWS

EXCELSIOR SPRINGS

■ Worrying squirrels is not tolerated.

■ Women are prohibited from wearing corsets because 'the privilege of admiring the curvaceous, unencumbered body of a young woman should not be denied to the normal, red-blooded American male'.

KANSAS CITY

■ Minors are not allowed to buy cap pistols, but can freely purchase shotguns.

MARCELINE

■ Minors are allowed to purchase cigarette paper and tobacco, but not lighters.

MARQUETTE

- In accordance with the brothel law, it is against the law for more than four unrelated persons to live in the same house/flat.

MOLE

- It is a violation of the law to frighten a baby.

ST LOUIS

- A milkman may not run while on duty.

- Farting in church carries a mandatory life sentence.

- It's illegal to sit on the kerb of any city street and drink beer from a bucket.

Montana

STATE LAWS

■ It is unlawful for a man and a woman to have sex in any position other than the missionary position.

■ It is illegal for married women to go fishing alone on Sundays, and illegal for single women to fish alone at all.

■ It is a felony for a wife to open her husband's mail.

■ All sexual activity between members of the opposite sex is banned in the front yard of a home after sunset – if they're nude.

■ A woman cannot dance on a table in a saloon or bar unless she has on at least 3lbs 2oz of clothing.

Nebraska

STATE LAWS

- A parent can be arrested if his/her child cannot hold back a burp during a church service.

- A mother cannot give her daughter a perm without a state licence.

CITY LAWS

HASTINGS

- Owners of every hotel are required to provide each guest with a clean and pressed nightshirt. No couple, even if they are married, may sleep together in the nude; nor may they have sex unless they are wearing a clean, white, cotton nightshirt.

WATERLOO

- Barbers are not allowed to eat onions between 7 a.m. and 7 p.m.

New Hampshire

- You may not tap your feet, nod your head, or in any way keep time to the music in a restaurant or café.

- Individuals cannot sell the clothes they are wearing to pay off a gambling debt.

- Any cattle that cross state roads must be fitted with a contraption to gather their faeces.

- On Sundays citizens may not look up while relieving themselves.

New Jersey

STATE LAWS

- It is against the law to 'frown' at a police officer.

- It is a crime to delay or detain a homing pigeon.

- It is unlawful to feed whisky or offer cigarettes to animals at the local zoo.

CITY LAWS

CRESSKILL

- All cats must wear three bells to warn birds of their whereabouts.

LIBERTY CORNER

■ Lovers must avoid satisfying their lustful urges in a parked car. If the horn accidentally sounds while they are frolicking behind the wheel, the couple can face a jail term.

NEWARK

■ It is illegal to buy ice cream after 6 p.m. unless you have a written note from your doctor.

OCEAN CITY

■ Pinball machines are not to be played on Sundays.

■ Slurping soup is forbidden.

TRENTON

■ Pickles are not to be consumed on Sundays.

■ It is unlawful to throw away tainted pickles in the street.

Legal Laughs XII

Your attorney and your mother-in-law are trapped in a burning building. You only have time to save one of them.
Do you: (1) have lunch? or (2) go to the cinema?

❦

A housewife, an accountant and a lawyer were asked 'How much is two plus two?'

The housewife replied: 'Four!'

The accountant said: 'I think it's either three or four. Let me run those figures through my spreadsheet one more time.'

The lawyer drew the curtains, dimmed the lights and asked in a hushed voice, 'How much do you want it to be?'

❦

A lawyer and an engineer were fishing in the Caribbean. The lawyer said 'I'm here 'cause my house burned down and everything I owned was destroyed by the fire. The insurance company paid for everything.'

'That's quite a coincidence,' said the engineer. 'I'm here 'cause my house and all my belongings were destroyed by a flood, and my insurance company also paid for everything.'

The lawyer pondered the engineer's plight for a moment and, looking somewhat confused asked, 'How do you start a flood?'

New Mexico

STATE LAWS

■ It's forbidden for a female to appear unshaven in public.

■ Couples are allowed to have sex in a parked vehicle during their lunch break from work, as long as the car or van has drawn curtains to stop strangers from peeking in.

■ A newspaper can be fined if it misspells a person's name in print.

■ *Did you know:*
State officials in New Mexico ordered 400 words of 'sexually explicit material' to be cut from Romeo and Juliet.

CITY LAWS

CARRIZOZO

■ It's forbidden for females to appear unshaven in public (including legs and face).

LAS CRUCES

■ Individuals are not allowed to carry a lunchbox down Main Street.

New York

STATE LAWS

- A fine of $25 can be levied for flirting. This old law specifically prohibits men from looking 'at a woman in that way'.

- It is a crime to throw a ball at someone's head for fun.

- The penalty for jumping off a building is death.

- Slippers are not to be worn after 10 p.m.

- It's a crime to do anything against the law.

- You need a licence to use a clothesline outdoors.

- It is a crime to have nude dummies on display.

- Arresting a dead man for being in debt is forbidden.

CITY LAWS

CARMEL

- A man can't go outside while wearing a jacket and trousers that do not match.

GREENE

- It is against the law to eat peanuts and walk backwards on the pavement when a concert is on.

LIDENHURST

- It is illegal for a woman to give a man a perm.

NEW YORK CITY

- Women are not allowed to be on the street wearing 'body-hugging clothing'.
- You may not smile within 100 feet of the entrance to a public building.
- Women may go topless in public, providing it is not for business purposes.
- It's an offence to walk down the street reading.

WOODSTOCK

- It is illegal to walk your bear on the street without a lead.

North Carolina

STATE LAWS

- It is illegal to sing off key.
- Elephants may not be used to plough cotton fields.
- Whilst having sex, you must stay in the missionary position and have the blinds down.
- If an unmarried couple go to a hotel/motel and register themselves as married, then by state law they are legally married.
- Sexual intercourse in a churchyard is illegal.

CITY LAWS

BARBER

- Fights between cats and dogs are prohibited.

CHAPEL HILL

- It is a misdemeanour to urinate or defecate publicly.

CHARLOTTE

- Women must cover their bodies with at least 16 yards of cloth at all times.

North Dakota

STATE LAWS

- It is illegal to lie down and fall asleep with your shoes on.

- Beer and pretzels can't be served at the same time in any bar or restaurant.

- If a man accused of a crime refuses to accompany you to the police station, you are legally entitled to shoot him.

CITY LAWS

FARGO

- It is possible to be jailed for wearing a hat while dancing, or even for wearing a hat to a function where dancing is taking place.

Ohio

STATE LAWS

- Breast-feeding is not permitted in public.
- It is illegal to get a fish drunk.
- Using explosives when fishing is illegal.

CITY LAWS

BAY VILLAGE

- It is a crime to walk a cow down Lake Road.

BEXLEY

- The installation and usage of slot machines in outhouses is prohibited.

CLEVELAND

- It's illegal to catch mice without a hunting licence.
- Women are forbidden from wearing patent leather shoes, in case men see reflections of their underwear.

CLINTON COUNTY

- Any person found leaning against a public building will be subject to fines.

IRONTON

- Cross-dressing is against the law.

MARION

- It is a crime to eat a doughnut and walk backwards on a city street.

OXFORD

- It's illegal for a woman to strip off her clothing while standing in front of a man's picture.

PAULDING

- A policeman may bite a dog to quieten him down.

TOLEDO

- Throwing a snake at anyone is illegal.

XENIA

- It is illegal to spit in a salad bar.

Oklahoma

STATE LAWS

- Oklahoma will not tolerate anyone taking a bite out of another person's hamburger.

- It is illegal to put the hind legs of a farm animal in your boots.

- People who make ugly faces at dogs may be fined or jailed.

- Sex before marriage is forbidden.

- Fish may not be contained in fishbowls while on a public bus.

- Tissues must not be left in the back of one's car.

- Females are forbidden from doing their own hair without being licensed by the state.

- Dogs must have a permit signed by the mayor in order to congregate in groups of three or more on private property.

CITY LAWS

ADA

- If you wear New York Jets clothes you will be put into the state penitentiary.

CLINTON

- Molesting a car is against the law.

HARTSHORNE

- It is unlawful to put any hypnotized person in a display window.

OKLAHOMA CITY

- No one may walk backwards downtown while eating a hamburger.

- It is against the law to throw snowballs.

SCHULTER

- Women may not gamble in the nude, in lingerie, or while wearing a towel.

- You may not open a soft drink bottle without the supervision of a licensed engineer.

- Elephants are not to be taken into the downtown area.

WYNONA

- Mules may not drink out of bird-baths.

- Clothes may not be washed in bird-baths.

YUKON

- When you pass another car, you must beep your horn at them.

Oregon

STATE LAWS

- Dishes must be allowed to drip dry.
- It is illegal to whisper dirty things in your lover's ear during sex.

CITY LAWS

HOOD RIVER

- Juggling is strictly prohibited without a licence.

KLAMATH FALLS

- It's illegal to walk down a pavement and knock a snake's head off with your cane.
- People may not whistle under water.
- Roller skates must not be worn in public toilets.

SALEM

- Women are not allowed to wrestle.

STANFIELD

- It is against the law for animals to have sex in the city limits.

Pennsylvania

STATE LAWS

- A special cleaning ordinance bans housewives from hiding dirt and dust under a rug in a dwelling.

- No man may purchase alcohol without written consent from his wife.

- People are not allowed to sing in the bath.

- Firework stores may not sell fireworks to residents of the state.

- Fish must not be caught by any body part except the mouth.

- It is illegal for over 16 women to occupy a house together because that constitutes a brothel . . . however up to 120 men can live together without breaking the law.

- Cars travelling on country roads at night must send up a rocket every mile, then wait ten minutes for the road to clear.

- If a driver sees a team of horses he is to pull to one side of the road and cover his machine with a blanket or dust cover that has been painted to blend into the scenery.

- In the event that a horse refuses to pass a car on the road, the owner must take his car apart and conceal the parts in the bushes.

- Guns, cannons, revolvers or other explosive weapons must not be fired at a wedding.

CITY LAWS

ALLENTOWN

- There is a ban on men becoming aroused in public.
- All fire hydrants must be checked one hour before all fires.

ATLOONA

- A babysitter is not allowed to clean out his/her employer's fridge.

CONNELLSVILLE

- Trousers or jeans must never be worn so low that they reveal one's underwear.

MORRISVILLE

- Women must have a permit to wear cosmetics.

PITTSBURGH

- It is unlawful to sleep on a fridge.

TARENTUM

- Horses must not be tied to parking meters.

Legal Laughs XIII

While on holiday in Philadelphia, two young couples became acquainted and their two young sons struck up a friendship:

'My name is Billy. What's yours?' asked the first boy.

'Tommy,' replied the second.

'My Daddy's an accountant. What does your Daddy do for a living?' asked Billy.

Tommy replied, 'My Daddy's a lawyer.'

'Honest?' asked Billy.

'No, just the regular kind,' replied Tommy.

～～～

After her conviction of murder in the second degree, the District Attorney, during her sentencing hearing said, 'Mrs Packard – after you put the arsenic in the stew and served it to your husband, didn't you feel even a little remorse for what you were doing?'

'I did,' she said calmly.

'And when was that?' quipped the D.A.

'When he asked for seconds!'

Rhode Island

NEWPORT

■ Smoking a pipe after sunset is prohibited.

PROVIDENCE

■ It is against the law to wear transparent clothing.

WEST WARWICK

■ It is a crime to use water on even-numbered days for the sole purpose of watering the garden; if this law is broken there is a fine of $25-$100.

SOUTH CAROLINA

STATE LAWS

■ It is a capital offence to kill someone accidentally while attempting suicide.

■ It is considered an offence to get a tattoo.

■ It is illegal to crawl around the public sewer system without a written permit from the relevant authority.

CITY LAWS

CHARLESTON

- The Fire Department has the authority to blow up anyone's house.

- A prisoner may be charged a dollar for the journey to jail.

LANCASTER COUNTY

- Dancing in public is not allowed.

SPARTANBURG

- It is an offence to eat watermelons in the Magnolia Street cemetery.

South Dakota

STATE LAWS

- It is an offence to lie down and fall asleep in a cheese factory.

- If there are more than five Native Americans on your property you may shoot them.

- Teenagers caught smoking can be fined for every cigarette they light.

CITY LAWS

SIOUX FALLS

■ Every hotel room is required to have twin beds; the beds must always be a minimum of two feet apart when a couple rents a room for only one night; and it's illegal to make love on the floor between the beds.

SPEARFISH

■ If three or more Native American Indians are walking down the street together, they can be considered a war party and shot at.

Tennessee

STATE LAWS

■ You can't shoot any game other than whales from a moving car.

■ Lassos must not be used to catch fish.

■ Driving is not to be done while asleep.

■ The age of consent is 16 years, but if the girl is a virgin it is 12 years.

■ No woman shall operate a car unless a man is running or walking in front of the car waving a red flag to warn approaching pedestrians and motorists.

CITY LAWS

DYERSBURG

■ It is illegal for a woman to call a man for a date.

MEMPHIS

■ Frogs are not allowed to croak after 11 p.m.

■ If you sell hollow logs you are breaking the law.

ONEIDA

■ An ordinance forbids anyone to sing the song 'It Ain't Goin' To Rain No More'.

Did you know?
Under new legislation, children now need parental consent in order to get their navels pierced in Tennessee.

Texas

STATE LAWS

- It is a crime to take more than three sips of beer at a time while standing.

- It is illegal for one to shoot a buffalo from the second storey of a hotel.

- A city ordinance states that a person cannot go barefoot without first obtaining a special five-dollar permit.

- It is a crime to milk or put graffiti on another person's cow.

- The entire *Encyclopaedia Britannica* is banned because it contains a formula for making beer at home.

- One must never curse in front of or indecently expose a corpse.

- It's legal for a chicken to have sex with you, but it's illegal to reciprocate.

- When two trains meet at a railroad crossing both must come to a stop. Then neither train may continue until the other one is out of sight.

- The act of breaking wind in a lift is unlawful.

CITY LAWS

CLARENDON

- Public buildings must not be dusted with feather dusters.

DALLAS

■ The possession of realistic dildos is forbidden.

HOUSTON

■ It is a crime to buy beer after midnight on a Sunday, but it can be bought on a Monday.

MESQUITE

■ It is unlawful for children to have unusual haircuts.

PORT ARTHUR

■ Obnoxious odours may not be emitted while in a lift.

SAN ANTONIO

■ It is a crime to urinate on the Alamo.

TEMPLE

■ You can ride your horse in the saloon.
■ Cattle thieves may be hung on the spot.

TEXARKANA

■ Horses can only be ridden at night if they are wearing taillights.

Legal Laughs XIV

A Mexican bandit made a habit of crossing the Rio Grande, expressly to rob banks in Texas. Finally, a reward was offered for his capture, DEAD or ALIVE! A trigger-happy, enterprising, young Texas Ranger decided to track down the bandit on his own and collect the reward. After a lengthy search, the Ranger tracked the bandit to his favourite cantina and snuck up behind him. At the sound of the Ranger's guns cocking and preparing to fire, the surprised bandit sped around only to see both of the Ranger's six-shooters bearing down on him.

The Ranger announced, 'You're under arrest! Tell me where you hid the loot or I'll drop you where you stand,' his finger becoming itchy on the trigger.

However, the bandit didn't speak English and the Ranger didn't speak Spanish. Fortunately for the Ranger, a bilingual lawyer was present in the cantina and translated the Ranger's demand to the bandit. The terrified bandit blurted out, in Spanish, that the loot was buried next to an old oak tree behind the cantina.

'What did he say, what did he say?' the Ranger hurriedly asked. To which the lawyer replied,

'Well, the best I can make out he said ... *Draw*!'

Utah

STATE LAWS

- It is illegal not to drink milk.

- It is a crime to detonate any nuclear weapon; citizens can own them, but just not set them off.

- Birds have the right of way on all highways.

- No one may have sex in the back of an ambulance if it is responding to an emergency.

CITY LAWS

LOGAN

- Woman are not allowed to swear.

MONROE

- Daylight must be visible between partners on a dance floor.

PROVO

- Throwing snowballs is against the law and anyone caught could face a $50 fine.

SALT LAKE CITY

- No one may walk down the street carrying a paper bag containing a violin.

TREMONTON

■ No woman may have sex with a man while riding in an ambulance within the boundaries. If she was caught the woman could be charged and her name printed in the local paper; the man's identity would not be revealed and nor would he be charged.

Vermont

STATE LAWS

■ It is unlawful to sell horse urine without a licence.

■ It is illegal to deny the existence of God.

■ Women must obtain written permission from their husbands to wear false teeth.

Virginia

STATE LAWS

■ You can't have sex with the lights on or in any position other than the missionary.

■ Police radar detectors are unlawful.

■ It is illegal to tickle women.

CITY LAWS

CULPEPER

- Mules must not be washed on the pavement.

NORFOLK

- A hen cannot lay eggs before 8 a.m. or after 4 p.m.

- A woman cannot go out without wearing a corset.

- Hunting with a rifle is lawful as long as the hunter is 50 feet off the ground.

- Spitting on seagulls is forbidden.

RICHMOND

- It's unlawful to toss a coin in a restaurant to see who pays for the coffee.

WAYNESBORO

- It is illegal for a woman to drive a car up Main Street unless her husband is walking in front of the vehicle with a flag.

Legal Laughs XV

A bored truck driver had a nasty habit of swerving to hit attorneys he found walking alongside the highway. One day as he was driving along he came across a nun who appeared to be having car trouble. Pulling over he offered the nun a ride to the nearest service station, and the nun graciously thanked him for stopping and accepted his offer. After driving a few miles the truck driver saw an attorney walking along the highway. As was his custom, the truck driver swerved to hit the attorney but, at the last moment, remembered he had the nun as a passenger and abruptly swerved away to avoid hitting him. However, upon hearing a loud 'thump', the truck driver peered in his rear-view mirror only to see the attorney lying injured on the side of the road.

'I'm so sorry Sister, I thought I missed hitting that attorney!' the truck driver pleaded.

'You did my son, but I got him with the door!' said the nun gleefully.

⌘

A plaintiff lawyer had a jury trial in a very difficult business case. The client who had attended the trial was out of town when the jury came back with its decision. Verdict for Plaintiff!

The lawyer immediately sent a telegram to his client, reading 'Justice has triumphed!' The client immediately wired back, 'Appeal at once!'

Washington

STATE LAWS

- All lollipops are banned.

- A law to reduce crime states: 'It is mandatory for a motorist with criminal intentions to stop and telephone the chief of police as he is entering the town.'

- It is unlawful to paint polka dots on the American flag.

- It is a crime to pretend that one's parents are rich.

CITY LAWS

AUBURN

- Men found guilty of deflowering virgins, regardless of age or marital status, may face up to five years imprisonment.

BELLINGHAM

- An old law made it a crime for a woman to take more than three steps backwards while dancing.

EVERETT

- It is illegal to display a hypnotized or allegedly hypnotized person in a store window.

LYNDEN

- Dancing and drinking must not occur at the same venue.

SEATTLE

- You may not carry a concealed weapon that is over six feet in length.

- Women who sit on a man's lap on buses or trains without placing a pillow between their bodies face an automatic twelve-month jail sentence.

- Fishbowls and aquariums are not allowed on city buses because the sound of sloshing might disturb other passengers.

SPOKANE

- It is legal to buy a radio on the Sabbath but illegal to buy a television.

- It is illegal for a racehorse to interrupt a religious meeting.

WILBUR

- You may not ride an ugly horse through the streets.

West Virginia

STATE LAWS

- Children are not allowed to attend school with their breath smelling of wild onions.

- It is not a crime for a male to have sex with an animal as long as it does not exceed 40 lbs.

- It is illegal to snooze on a train.

- A man can only marry his first cousin if she is under the age of 55.

- Roadkill may be picked up and taken home for supper.

CITY LAWS

HUNTINGTON

- Firemen are not allowed to flirt with or whistle at any woman passing a fire station.

NICHOLAS COUNTY

- No member of the clergy is allowed to tell jokes or humorous stories from the pulpit during a church service.

Wisconsin

STATE LAWS

- Citizens may not murder their enemies.

- According to state law it is illegal to serve apple pie in public restaurants without cheese.

- Kissing on a train is forbidden.

- It is a crime to cut a woman's hair.

CITY LAWS

CONNORSVILLE

- It's unlawful for a man to shoot off a gun when his female partner has an orgasm.

RACINE

- Firemen must not be woken up when they are asleep.

ST CROIX

- Women are not allowed to wear anything red in public.

Legal Laughs XVI

A stranger walked into the local Chamber of
Commerce of a small town, obviously desperate.
Seeing a man at the counter, the stranger asked,
'Is there a criminal attorney in town?'

The man behind the counter immediately
quipped, 'Yes, but we can't prove it yet!'

～～～

A lawyer charged a client £500 for legal services.
The client paid him with crisp new £50 notes.
After the client left, the lawyer discovered that
two of the notes had stuck together – he'd been
overpaid by £50. The ethical dilemma for the
lawyer: should he tell his partner?

～～～

A man walked into a lawyer's office and enquired
about the lawyer's rates.

'£50 for three questions,' replied the lawyer.

'Isn't that pretty steep?' asked the man while
doling out the £50.

'Yes,' answered the lawyer. 'What's your third
question?'

Wyoming

STATE LAWS

- Women are not allowed to stand within five feet of a bar while drinking.

- You may not take a picture of a rabbit during the month of June.

CITY LAWS

CHEYENNE

- Citizens may not take a shower on a Wednesday.

NEWCASTLE

- Couples are forbidden from having sex while standing inside a store's walk-in meat freezer.

Stupid Laws of South America

Bolivia

CITY LAWS

SANTA CRUZ

- It is illegal for a man to have sex with a woman and her daughter at the same time.

Colombia

CITY LAWS

CALI

■ A woman is only permitted to have sex with her husband and the first time this happens her mother must be in the room to witness the act.

CUBA

■ It is a criminal offence to insult the dignity of a public official.

> *Did you know?*
> *In Cuba, it is a crime to be a 'dangerous person' even if a suspect has not violated any other law. Cuban law defines 'dangerousness' (el estado peligross) as 'the special proclivity of a person to commit crimes, demonstrated by conduct that is observed to be in manifest contradiction with the norms of socialist morality'.*

Mexico

CITY LAWS

AGUASCALIENTES

■ Any form of nude artistic display is unlawful.

GUADALAJARA

■ It is a crime to shout offensive words in public.

■ During office hours, women who work for the city government must not wear mini skirts or other garments deemed to be 'provocative'.

Legal Laughs XVII

After his motion to suppress evidence was denied by the court the attorney spoke up, 'Your Honour,' he said. 'What would you do if I called you a stupid, degenerate, old fool?'

The judge, in angry tones, responded, 'I would hold you in contempt of court and seek to have you suspended from practising before this court again!'

'What if I only thought it?' asked the attorney.

'In that case, there is nothing I could do, you have the right to think whatever you may,' said the judge.

'Oh, I see. Then, if it pleases the court, let the record reflect, I "think" you're a stupid, degenerate, old fool.'

∽∼∾∾

A defendant was asked if he wanted a bench trial or a jury trial. 'Jury trial,' he replied.

'Do you understand the difference?' asked the judge.

'Sure,' replied the defendant. 'That's where twelve ignorant people decide my fate instead of one.'

∽∼∾∾

An attorney, addressing the jury and speaking of his client who recently killed his parents:

'Dear ladies and gentlemen, please take mercy and release this poor orphan.'

Stupid Laws
of Africa

East Africa

■ In some parts of the region, a man seen carrying an unrelated woman on his bicycle can be convicted of adultery, as long as the act is witnessed by enough people.

■ If a husband discovers a man *in flagrante delicto* with his wife, this will not constitute admissible evidence – he will have to bring in other witnesses which, unless the adulterous act was unusually public, will not be possible.

Morocco

■ Anyone accompanying someone who possesses illegal drugs, even if they are unaware that their companion is carrying them, can be tried for the same crime.

Nigeria

■ It is an offence under the Army Colour (Protection of Use) Act 1990 to drive a car painted in the same shade of green used by the army.

South Africa

■ A statute provides that during a tenancy, a labour tenant may use manure for cultivating fields lawfully occupied by him, but he is not allowed to sell or give it to a third party. The manure is the property of the landowner who, the law stipulates, 'may vindicate it in the hands of the third party' even if the latter had purchased it in good faith.

Legal Laughs XVIII

The following are actual statements found on insurance forms where car drivers summarized the details of their accident as briefly as possible.

Coming home I drove into the wrong house and collided with a tree I don't have.

The other car collided with mine without giving any warning of its intentions.

A pedestrian hit me and went under my car.

The guy was all over the road. I had to swerve a number of times before I hit him.

I pulled away from the side of the road, glanced at my mother-in-law, and headed over an embankment.

In my attempt to kill a fly, I drove into a telephone pole.

I had been shopping for plants all day and was on my way home. As I reached an intersection, a hedge sprang up, obscuring my vision and I did not see the other car.

The pedestrian had no idea which way to run, so I ran over him.

As I approached an intersection a sign suddenly appeared in a place where no stop sign had ever appeared before. I was unable to stop in time to avoid the accident.

To avoid hitting the bumper of the car in front, I struck the pedestrian.

My car was legally parked as it backed into the other vehicle.

The telephone pole was approaching. I was attempting to swerve out of its way when it struck the front of my car.

Now you can order superb titles directly from **Michael O'Mara Books**.

The One Hundred Stupidest Things Ever Done	Ross & Kathryn Petras	£3.99
The Stupidest Things Ever Said	Ross & Kathryn Petras	£3.99
Stupid Movie Lines	Ross & Kathryn Petras	£3.99
Stupid Sex	Ross & Kathryn Petras	£3.99
Stupid Things Men Do		£3.99
The World's Stupidest Signs		£3.99
The Little Book of Farting	Alec Bromcie	£1.99
The Complete Book of Farting	Alec Bromcie	£4.99

Please allow for postage and packing:
UK: free delivery
Europe: add 20% of retail price
Rest of World: add 30% of retail price

To order any of the above or any other Michael O'Mara titles, please call our credit card orderline or fill in this coupon and send / fax to:

Michael O'Mara Books, 250 Western Avenue, London W3 6EE, UK
Telephone 020 8324 5652 Facsimile 020 8324 5678

I enclose a UK bank cheque made payable to MOM Bookshop Ltd for £_____

Please charge £ _____ to my Access/Visa/Delta/Switch

Card No. _____

Expiry date: _____ Switch Issue No. _____

NAME (Block Letters please): _____

ADDRESS: _____

_____

_____POSTCODE:_____

TELEPHONE: _____

SIGNATURE: _____